THE STORY OF MAYA ANGELOU

A Biography Book for New Readers

— Written by —
Tiffany Obeng

— Illustrated by —
Rahana Dariah

ROCKRIDGE PRESS

> Dr. Maya Angelou loved everyone as if they were her true children. So, this book is dedicated to all of her children, and that includes you. May you be inspired to love like Dr. Angelou, hope like Dr. Angelou, and never give up.

Copyright © 2023 by Rockridge Press

All rights reserved. No part of this publication may be reproduced, stored in a retrieval system, or transmitted in any form or by any means, electronic, mechanical, photocopying, recording, scanning, or otherwise, without the prior written permission of the Publisher. Requests to the Publisher for permission should be addressed to the Permissions Department, Rockridge Press, 1955 Broadway, Suite 400, Oakland, CA 94612.

First Rockridge Press trade paperback edition 2023

Rockridge Press and the Rockridge Press logo are trademarks or registered trademarks of Callisto Media Inc. and/or its affiliates in the United States and other countries and may not be used without written permission.

For general information on our other products and services, please contact our Customer Care Department within the United States at (866) 744-2665, or outside the United States at (510) 253-0500.

Paperback ISBN: 979-8-88650-822-2 | eBook ISBN: 979-8-88650-835-2

Manufactured in the United States of America

Series Designer: Angela Navarra
Interior and Cover Designer: Brieanna H. Felschow
Art Producer: Sue Bischofberger
Editor: Eliza Kirby
Production Editor: Melissa Edeburn
Production Manager: David Zapanta

Illustrations © 2022 Rahana Dariah
Photography © Everett Collection Historical / Alamy Stock Photo, p. 50; © Tom Croke / Alamy Stock Photo, p. 52; © Olivier Douliery/ABACAPRESS.COM / Alamy Stock Photo, p. 53. Author photo courtesy of Bayo Fame
Maps used under license from Creative Market

10 9 8 7 6 5 4 3 2 1

CONTENTS

CHAPTER 1 A Poet Is Born	1
CHAPTER 2 The Early Years	7
CHAPTER 3 The Power of Words	15
CHAPTER 4 A Gifted Artist	22
CHAPTER 5 A Powerful Voice	29
CHAPTER 6 A Famous Writer	36
CHAPTER 7 A Prize-Winning Poet	43
CHAPTER 8 So... Who Was Maya Angelou?	50
GLOSSARY	56
BIBLIOGRAPHY	58

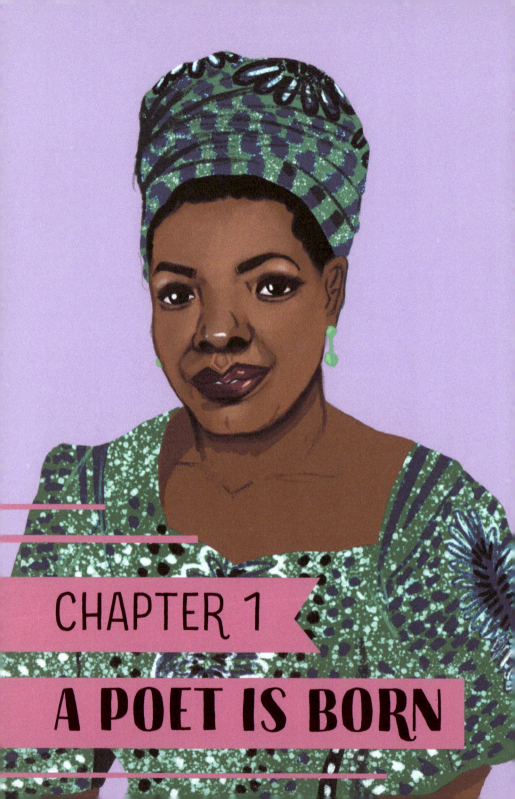

★ Meet Maya Angelou ★

Ring-ring! Maya Angelou's phone rang. She answered it. "Yes, I can do that," Maya replied quickly. The call ended and Maya realized what she had done. She had just agreed to write a poem and read it at the upcoming **inauguration** of the 42nd president of the United States. Maya Angelou would be only the second poet to ever read a poem at a presidential inauguration. She would be the first Black poet and the first female poet to do so!

Maya was nervous. She wondered if she could do it. Maya wrote and practiced every day. She could not let the president down. Then, on that sunny, cool day, January 20, 1993, Maya rose from her seat. She was 64 years old. She stood tall at six feet. She walked to the podium and

---

JUMP —IN THE— THINK TANK

What talent could the president ask you to share? How would you prepare for a major performance?

laid her poem down. She wrapped her long fingers around the edges of the podium to calm herself. She looked out at the enormous, quiet crowd, trying not to think of the millions more watching on TV. She raised her head high and she opened her mouth. In her deep, powerful voice, Maya began her poem. "A Rock, A River, A Tree..."

When Maya finished, the crowd cheered. Maya had done what she always had. She had spread a message of hope and kindness.

⭐ Maya's America ⭐

On April 4, 1928, Maya Angelou was born Marguerite Annie Johnson in St. Louis, Missouri. Her mother was Vivian Baxter. Her father was Bailey Johnson Sr. Maya also had an older brother, Bailey Jr.

In 1928, St. Louis was filled with factories that made all sorts of things, from clothes to shoes to car parts and more. These factories burned coal to make their products. The burning made thick smoke called *smog* that filled the St. Louis sky. Sometimes the smog even blocked out the sun.

St. Louis also had plenty of playgrounds and parks where children could gather and play. The St. Louis Zoo, the Jefferson National Expansion Memorial, (now called Gateway Arch **National Park**), and the St. Louis Public Library were popular family pastimes.

St. Louis was home to a small, tight-knit community of Black people. Most had moved from other Southern states because **segregation** was not as harsh in St. Louis. Black and white people were allowed to attend common places and sit together

> You may not control all the events that happen to you, **but you can decide** not to be reduced by them.

on streetcars. Black people were safer there. They also had better jobs and housing opportunities.

Life in St. Louis for Black people seemed promising. But just one year after Maya's birth, the nation was struck by the **Great Depression**. During this time, businesses failed. It was hard to find work or make money. Black people had already been making less money than white people. Now they did not have jobs. Many lost their homes. Maya and her parents struggled just to live.

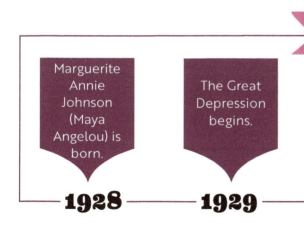

WHEN?

Marguerite Annie Johnson (Maya Angelou) is born. — **1928**

The Great Depression begins. — **1929**

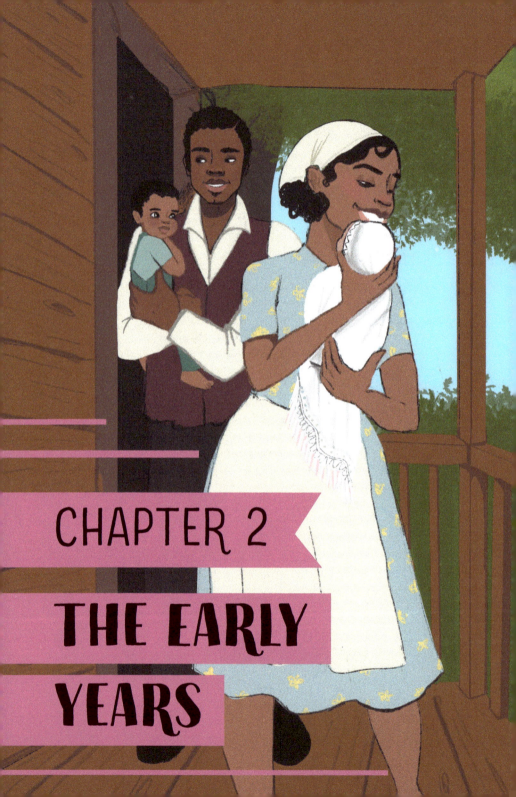

CHAPTER 2

THE EARLY YEARS

⭐ **From Missouri to Arkansas** ⭐

Maya's mother, Vivian, was beautiful, well-educated, and from a well-known family. She worked as a nurse. Maya's father, Bailey Sr., was a big man with wide shoulders. Though he was born in Trinidad, he loved being American. He worked as an apartment doorman.

But her brother was Maya's favorite person. Bailey was handsome with smooth dark skin and black curly hair. Unable to say Marguerite, toddler Bailey sweetly called his new sister "My-a-sister." Soon, Vivian and Bailey Sr. started calling their daughter Maya, too.

The Great Depression was tough on families. Vivian and Bailey Sr. began to have problems. They decided it was best to separate. They felt they could not care for Maya and Bailey while they were apart. Maya and Bailey instead went to live with their father's mother in Stamps, Arkansas.

Bailey Sr. dropped off three-year-old Maya and four-year-old Bailey at the train station. They only had the clothes they wore, wrist tags that said their names and destination, and each other.

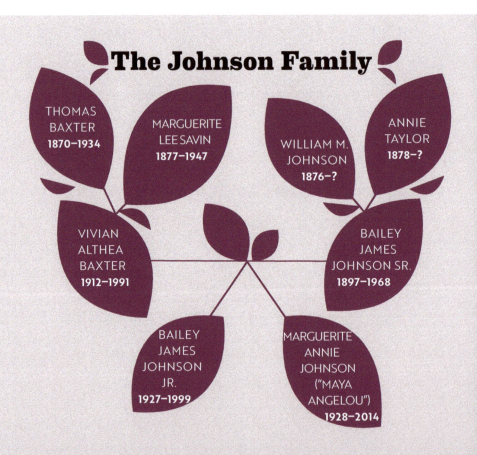

MYTH &	FACT
Maya and Bailey taking the train alone was very unusual.	Black children commonly traveled across the United States alone in the 1930s.

The **porter** looked after Maya and Bailey until the next day. He pinned their tickets to the inside of Bailey's coat pocket and got off in Arizona. Maya and Bailey were alone and scared.

Luckily, kind Black passengers cared for them. They offered the children cold fried chicken and potato salad from their lunch boxes. After a few days, Maya and Bailey finally arrived in Arkansas.

★ Momma's House ★

Stamps was different from St. Louis. There were no factories or endless playgrounds, just roads.

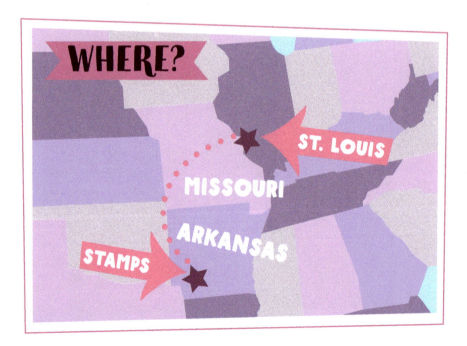

White people lived on one side of the town and Black people lived on the other.

Maya's grandmother, Annie "Momma" Henderson, owned the only store in the Black neighborhood. On Saturdays, the front porch became a barbershop and a resting place for people passing through.

Maya and Bailey lived in the back of the store with Momma and their Uncle Willie. Momma woke Maya and Bailey early every morning to help in the store. Maya and Bailey checked out customers and became extremely good at math. Maya enjoyed using her hand as a measuring cup to scoop flour into customers' small paper bags.

Momma taught Maya and Bailey Christian values. She insisted they always be **prudent** and

> **JUMP -IN THE- THINK TANK**
>
> Do you have any chores? How do you help around the house?

clean. On the coldest winter days, they still had to go outside to wash their bodies in the freezing well water. Momma also insisted they go to church every Sunday.

Uncle Willie taught them multiplication before kindergarten. He also gave them books to read. Stamps is where Maya fell in love with reading and words. Momma encouraged Maya, calling her "little professor."

Maya and Bailey grew close in Stamps. They read and played together. Other children in their neighborhood said mean things about the way Maya looked. Even adults joined in sometimes. It made Maya sad, but Bailey always cheered her up and defended her. Maya was thankful for Bailey.

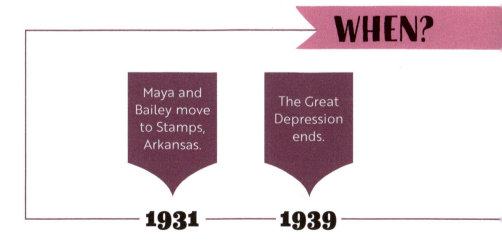

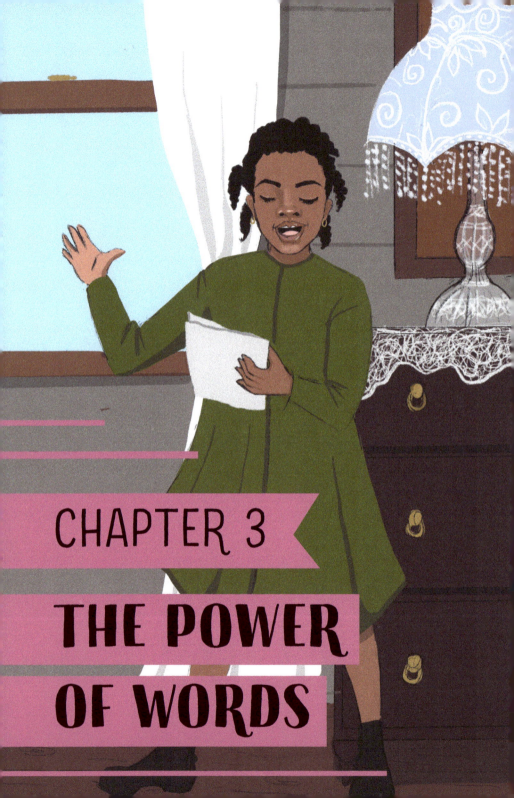

✦ Going Quiet ✦

After four years, Bailey Sr. unexpectedly came to get Maya and Bailey. He took them to St. Louis to live with Vivian. Maya cried the whole ride.

When they arrived, Maya and Bailey first lived in a big house with their Grandmother Baxter and their three uncles for six months. Then Maya and Bailey lived with Vivian and her boyfriend, Mr. Freeman. Moving often seemed natural for Maya's hectic life.

Life in St. Louis was so different. Maya and Bailey each had their own rooms and plenty of store-bought clothes. They ate new foods and learned to dance. They were the smartest children in their grades. They even skipped a grade.

JUMP —IN THE— THINK TANK

Maya found happiness in reading. What things do you like to do that make you happy or calm?

Maya spent her Saturdays at the library. But one Saturday, when Maya was eight, Mr. Freeman hurt her badly. He told her not to tell anyone or he would hurt Bailey, too. Maya stayed in bed for days. Her mother cared for her, and Bailey read to her.

Bailey begged Maya to tell him who hurt her. Maya finally told Bailey and Bailey wept. Bailey told Grandmother Baxter what happened. Mr. Freeman was arrested. Shortly after, he died.

So much had happened in such a short time. It made Maya very sad. Maya stopped talking to everyone, except Bailey. Adults misunderstood Maya's silence. They thought she was being rude or disobedient. After a year in St. Louis, Bailey and a silent Maya were on a train to Arkansas, back to Momma.

✦ Finding Flowers ✦

Feeling sad and unwanted, Maya was **mute** for the next five years. She only read books and took in her surroundings. She still went to school, but she never spoke in class. She turned in all her classwork in writing.

One summer afternoon, a woman named Mrs. Flowers invited Maya to her home. Mrs. Flowers was beautiful, poised, well-dressed, and well-educated. She was the richest woman on the Black side of Stamps. Maya admired Mrs. Flowers because Mrs. Flowers was different from any woman she had met. Seeing Mrs. Flowers made Maya proud to be Black.

Mrs. Flowers offered Maya lemonade and cookies baked specially for her. Mrs. Flowers read to Maya. Maya was in awe of Mrs. Flowers's poetic voice. She taught Maya about the value of language and the power of speaking words aloud. Mrs. Flowers taught Maya other important life lessons, like to be understanding of people who were unable to go to school.

MYTH	&	FACT
Children who can read on their own should read silently.		Reading aloud helps build confidence, memory, and speech.

She said those same people could be just as smart as college professors.

Mrs. Flowers gave Maya books to borrow, including a book of poems. Maya had never read poetry before. When Maya read poetry for the first time, she knew that she loved it. Poetry said the things that Maya felt.

Mrs. Flowers invited Maya back again and again.

> I was liked, and what a **difference it made**.

Mrs. Flowers's full attention made Maya feel liked and special. This gave Maya confidence. At age 12, Maya began speaking again. Maya and

Mrs. Flowers read books to each other. Maya memorized poems and recited them to Mrs. Flowers. Maya graduated from eighth grade with a new friend and at the top of her class.

WHEN?

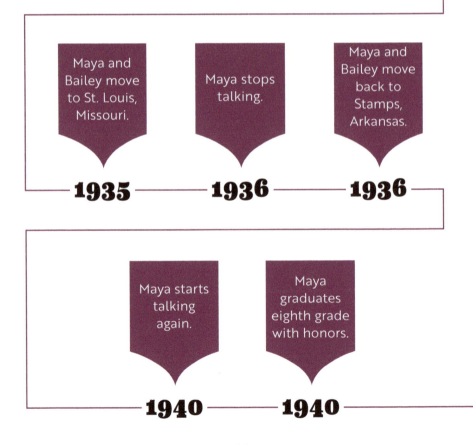

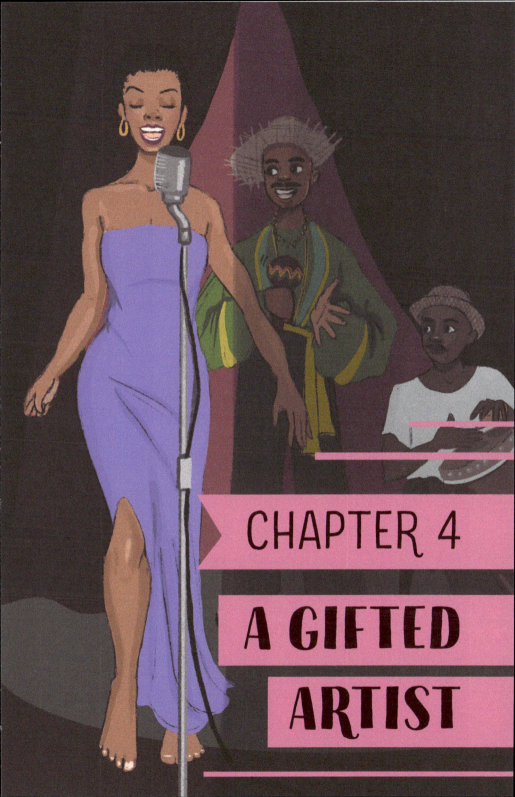

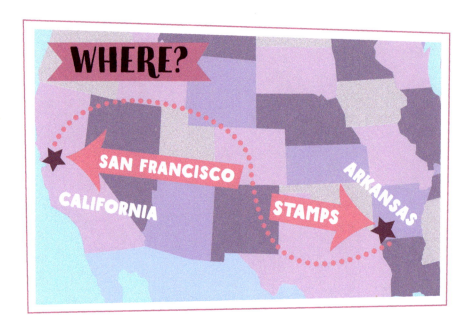

⭐ Becoming Angelou ⭐

After eighth grade, Maya and Bailey moved to San Francisco, California, with Vivian. Many other Black people were moving to San Francisco around the same time. World War II had created a lot of factory jobs there. Maya loved that San Francisco was full of newcomers like herself. She finally felt she belonged.

During high school, Maya earned a **scholarship** to take evening drama and dance classes.

Dancing helped Maya overcome her shyness. With her new confidence, Maya set out to become a streetcar conductor. Because the men were at war, women were allowed to fill these positions. No Black person had ever been a conductor, and at 16, Maya was too young to work. She did not let that stop her. After weeks of rejection, Maya made history as the first Black streetcar conductor in San Francisco.

Even though she was busy, Maya continued to do well in high school. At age 17, Maya became the first high school graduate in her family.

She later welcomed a precious son, Guy. Maya worked hard to support herself and her child. She worked as a cook, a waitress, and a music store clerk. Maya met Tosh Angelos, a Greek man, at the music store. They bonded over music and his kindness toward Guy. They married in 1951, just three years after **interracial marriage** became legal in California.

Maya kept taking dance classes during her marriage. After Maya and Tosh divorced in 1954, Maya found work as a professional dancer and singer. She took on the stage name Maya Angelou.

✦ A Performer and Writer ✦

In San Francisco, audiences loved Maya's long legs, tall height, and deep singing voice. She even performed songs made up from her very own poems. Maya was a regular feature in newspapers, guest on the radio, and performer on TV.

Her celebrity went beyond San Francisco. In 1954, Maya joined the historic all-Black cast of the stage play *Porgy and Bess* on an **international** tour. The show was the first to have mostly Black performers. *Porgy and Bess* gave Black singers the opportunity to perform on important stages where they had once been banned.

Maya traveled to 22 countries on tour. She learned to speak Italian, French, and **Serbo-Croatian**. Maya loved performing with her friends before sold-out audiences. Every **standing ovation** brought Maya joy. But she really missed her son back home.

MYTH & FACT
Maya Angelou was only a talented writer.
Maya was also a talented singer, dancer, and speaker.

JUMP —IN THE— THINK TANK

If you could travel anywhere in the world, where would you go?

Maya returned home after a year of touring. She began to write sketches, song lyrics, and short stories. She asked famous writer John Killens what he thought of her writing. John thought Maya had "undeniable talent." He invited Maya to New York to join his organization of Black writers and thinkers, the **Harlem Writers Guild**. John was the only published Black author she knew. Maya trusted him.

WHEN?

1944 — Maya graduates from high school.

1945 — World War II ends.

1948 — Interracial marriage becomes legal in California.

Maya and Guy moved to New York City in 1959. Maya learned that writing required hard work and focus. Soon it paid off. A Cuban magazine called *Revolución* published a short story by Maya. Maya became a published writer for the first time.

1951	1954	1959
Maya marries Tosh Angelos.	Maya goes on tour with *Porgy and Bess*.	Maya moves to New York.

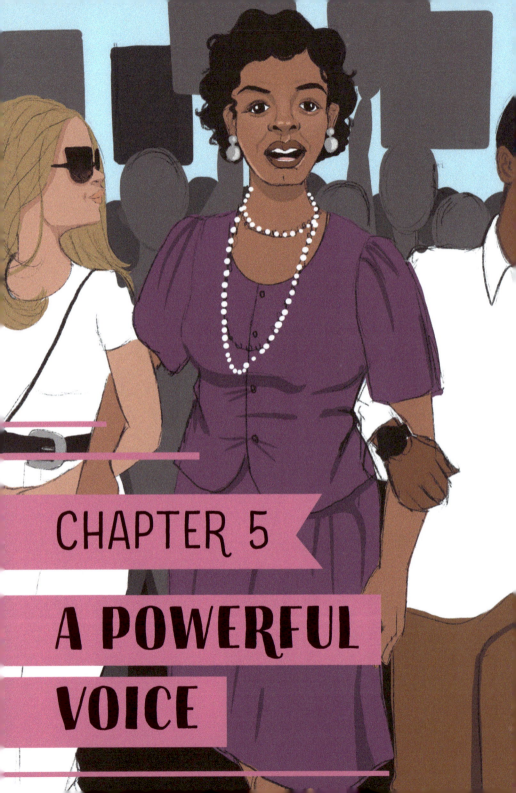

★ The Civil Rights Movement ★

In New York, Maya was surrounded by changemakers. She admired Black artists who used their art to raise awareness of racial injustice, like famous playwright Lorraine Hansberry. At the time, Black Americans were treated very differently from white Americans. Maya wanted to make art to support the **civil rights movement**.

In 1960, Maya and her friend comedian Godfrey Cambridge heard civil rights leader Dr. Martin Luther King Jr. speak. He was in New York to raise money for his organization, the Southern Christian Leadership Conference (SCLC). The SCLC organized protests and fought for equal rights for everyone.

" Human beings are more alike than unalike, and what is true anywhere is true everywhere. "

JUMP
—IN THE—
THINK TANK

Do you think everyone should be treated fairly? Why?

Martin preached that everyone was equal and responsible for one another. Maya and Godfrey were inspired to help. They planned a fundraiser, a show called *Cabaret for Freedom*. Maya called singers and dancers, wrote skits, and mailed announcements all over New York. Maya had never organized a fundraiser before. But she had purpose.

The show opened to a celebrity-filled audience and three standing ovations. It ran for five more weeks. It gave Black singers and dancers the opportunity to perform. It raised money for the SCLC. Soon after the cabaret closed, Maya took a position as regional coordinator for the SCLC.

Over the next year, Maya organized events to raise money for the SCLC. She sent out thousands of letters, signed invitations, and gave speeches. The money Maya raised allowed

Martin to travel across the United States and spread his message of racial equality. At their first meeting, Martin thanked Maya for her hard work.

★ Inspired by Her Travels ★

In 1961, Maya took her activism to Africa. In Cairo, Egypt, she worked with a civil rights organization. She and Guy learned to speak **Arabic**.

While there, Maya got a job, though women in Cairo did not typically work outside the home. With the help of a friend, journalist David

Dubois, Maya became the first female journalist for the political magazine *Arab Observer*. Her male coworkers were not very welcoming.

Maya was assigned to write about Africa. But Maya was American and had never been a journalist. Maya taught herself everything in two weeks. She read books about Africa and journalism. Maya worked hard and became a good journalist. Within a year, more female

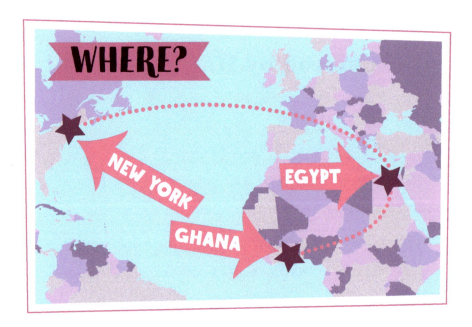

journalists were writing for the *Arab Observer*. Maya had paved the way.

Maya moved to Ghana in 1963. Practically everyone in Ghana was Black. It amazed Maya that Black people were pilots, doctors, and even the president. Maya looked forward to learning her sixth language, Fanti, and finding work.

Maya worked at the University of Ghana. She also continued to work as a journalist, this time for the *Ghanaian Times*. When civil rights activist Malcolm X visited Ghana, Maya helped him meet important Ghanaian officials.

Malcolm wrote to Maya often after his visit. He wrote about his new organization focused on uniting Black people with Africans. He urged Maya to return to America to run the organization and raise money, like she had done for Martin Luther King Jr. Maya accepted. She headed back to America in 1965.

WHEN?

1961 — Maya moves to Cairo, Egypt.

1962 — Maya becomes a journalist.

1963 — Maya moves to Ghana.

1965 — Maya returns to America.

MYTH	&	FACT
To be great at something, all you need is talent.		To be truly great at something, you must also work very hard.

⭐ Sharing Her Life ⭐

Malcolm X was **assassinated** just three days after Maya's return to America. His death greatly saddened Maya. She had lost a friend and her passion to help in the civil rights movement. She began performing again to feel less sad. Six months later, Maya realized that writing was her true passion. With her notebooks full of poems and the beginnings of a play, Maya moved from San Francisco back to New York in 1967. Maya focused on becoming a playwright and published poet.

In 1968, Maya agreed to take a break from writing and help Martin Luther King Jr. raise money for his latest cause. Maya planned to start a few days after her birthday. Shockingly, Martin was assassinated on Maya's birthday. Maya was devastated. She stayed at home for weeks.

One evening, Maya's friend James Baldwin, a famous writer, insisted Maya go with him to a dinner party. At the party, Maya shared stories of her childhood in Arkansas. Everyone loved her storytelling. They urged Maya to write a true story about her life—an **autobiography**.

Not many Black women writers had written about themselves before.

At the kitchen table with her pen and notebook, Maya started writing her life story.

She wrote about being left at the train station and her mute years. She wrote about Mrs. Flowers and reuniting with her mother.

She titled the book *I Know Why the Caged Bird Sings* after a line from a poem by Paul Laurence Dunbar. Maya's book was published in 1969. It became the first bestselling nonfiction book written by a Black woman. Like Maya, many people were raised by their grandmothers, had trouble speaking, or felt like outcasts.

Maya's story showed people they could not only survive, but they could thrive.

★ An Artist on the Rise ★

Maya was now a famous writer. Still, she continued to work hard. Maya published her first book of poetry in 1971. Her poems were about life as a Black woman in America. Maya's book of poetry was nominated for one of the highest awards for American writers, the Pulitzer Prize.

In 1972, Maya's screenplay *Georgia, Georgia* was made into a movie. Years earlier, Maya had tried and failed to find a **producer** for a different screenplay. Few producers would even read it. So, this was huge for Maya. It was also huge for Black women—Maya was the first Black woman screenwriter to have a movie produced.

JUMP –IN THE– THINK TANK

How would you feel if you really wanted to do something, but no one would help you? Would you give up or keep going?

Over the years, Maya wrote articles and short stories for magazines. She wrote and published more poems, including one of her most well-known poems, "Still I Rise." Maya wrote and published recipe books and children's books. She also finished her autobiographical series. Maya wrote and published seven autobiographies total. Few writers have written so many autobiographies.

Maya also returned to acting. She starred in plays and movies, like the six-part TV miniseries *Roots*. *Roots* was about the long-standing history and impact of **slavery** in America. More than half the

American population watched *Roots* when it aired in 1977. *Roots* remains one of the most successful TV miniseries of all time. Maya's hard work and talent in *Roots* earned her an Emmy nomination, one of the highest honors for TV actors.

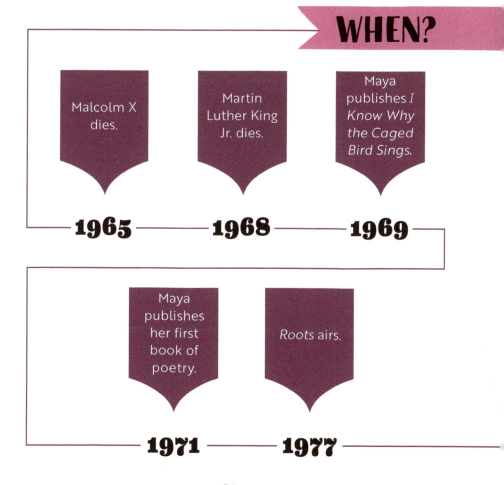

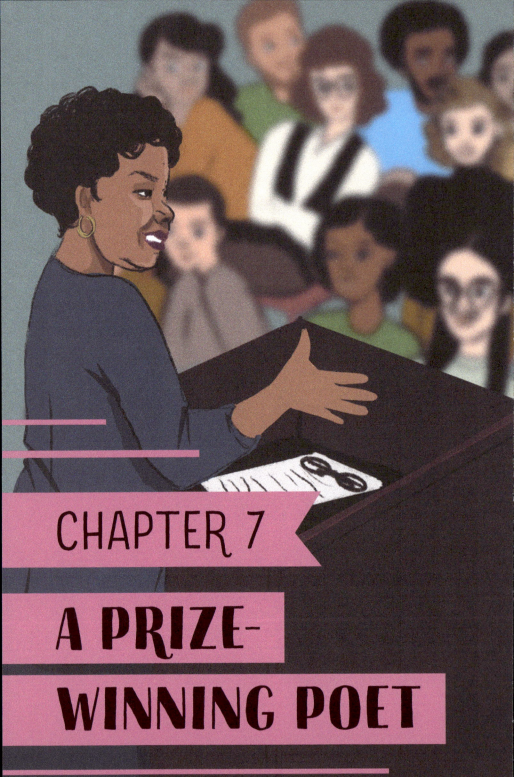

CHAPTER 7
A PRIZE-WINNING POET

⭐ The People's Poet ⭐

Maya had learned a lot over the years. By the 1980s, she was ready to teach. Maya took a job as a professor at Wake Forest University (WFU) in Winston-Salem, North Carolina. While most professors have a college degree, Maya had never gone to college. Instead, she was a successful performer, writer, and actress who had toured the world and fought for human rights. Maya's life experiences had taught her everything she knew.

As a professor, Maya shared the lessons she learned from Mrs. Flowers. For 32 years, she taught students the importance of writing and learning. Maya inspired courage, generosity, and love in them by being courageous, generous, and loving herself.

JUMP –IN THE– THINK TANK

We each have a message to share with the world. Maya's message was one of hope, love, and courage. What is your message?

In 1993, Maya inspired an entire nation to hope and love again when she recited her poem "On the Pulse of Morning" at the inauguration of President Bill Clinton. Before 800,000 people, Angelou became the second poet, the first Black person, and the first woman ever to read a poem at a presidential inauguration. The six-minute poem won Maya her first Grammy Award, the highest honor for poetry reading.

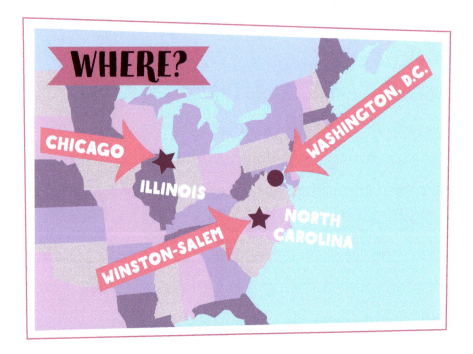

Maya developed many meaningful relationships over the years. One of her most special friendships was with famous television host Oprah Winfrey. They were friends for 20 years. Maya appeared on Oprah's show several times during its historic 25-year run, sharing her forever message of love, hope, and courage with a TV audience.

⭐ Maya's Legacy ⭐

On May 24, 2014, Oprah visited with Maya at Maya's home. "Love you, babe," Maya said to Oprah. "Love!" Oprah replied, and she left. It was a wonderful visit between friends. Three days later, Maya passed away. She was 86.

Heartfelt tributes from everyday people, celebrities, and global leaders filled the internet and TV screens. President Barack Obama honored Maya as "one of the brightest lights of our time." Former President Clinton honored Maya as "a national treasure." The world celebrated the life and loss of Maya.

> You can't use up creativity. The more you use, **the more you have.**

Despite a hard childhood, Maya grew up to become anything she wanted. She was a bold performer, a lifelong fighter for the rights of Black people and women, and an award-winning writer and poet who changed literature forever. She always tried and she never gave up. That was the amazing power of Maya.

Her first autobiography, *I Know Why the Caged Bird Sings,* is often removed from schools and libraries because it talks about difficult topics. The book continues to thrive anyway, just like Maya did. It is studied in many English classes today and remains Maya's most celebrated book.

Maya received countless awards and honors throughout her lifetime. She even received the National Medal of Arts, the highest honor for American artists. But Maya did not seek recognition. Maya wanted to be great, to help others be great, and to encourage people. Her positivity and wisdom carry on through her brilliant works and the generations of people she inspired.

WHEN?

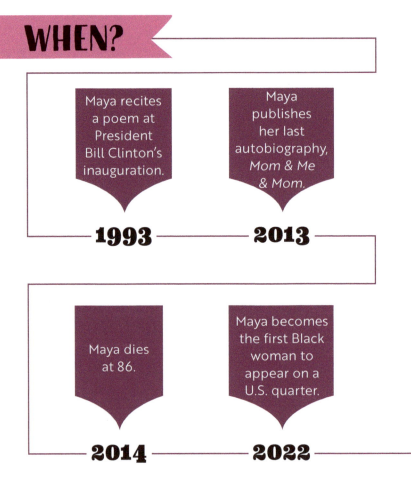

1993 — Maya recites a poem at President Bill Clinton's inauguration.

2013 — Maya publishes her last autobiography, *Mom & Me & Mom*.

2014 — Maya dies at 86.

2022 — Maya becomes the first Black woman to appear on a U.S. quarter.

CHAPTER 8

SO...WHO WAS MAYA ANGELOU?

★ Challenge Accepted! ★

Now that you know about Maya Angelou's life and work, let's test your new knowledge in a little who, what, when, where, why, and how quiz. Feel free to look back in the text to find the answers if you need to, but try to remember the answers first!

1 **Where was Maya born?**
→ A St. Louis
→ B California
→ C New York
→ D Arkansas

2 **What major event happened in the United States right after Maya was born?**
→ A World War I
→ B World War II
→ C Great Depression
→ D Great Resignation

50

3. Who was Grandmother "Momma" Henderson?

→ A   Maya's mother's mother
→ B   Maya's father's mother
→ C   Maya's aunt
→ D   Maya's favorite teacher

4. Why did Maya and her friend Godfrey plan *Cabaret for Freedom*?

→ A   Malcolm X asked them to
→ B   They were bored
→ C   They needed work
→ D   They wanted to help Martin Luther King Jr.

5. What is the name of the historic all-Black play that Maya toured with?

→ A   *Porgy and Bess*
→ B   *Dreamgirls*
→ C   *The Lion King*
→ D   *Wicked*

6 **When did Maya join the Harlem Writers Guild?**
→ A   1967
→ B   1991
→ C   2000
→ D   1959

7 **How many languages could Maya speak?**
→ A   1
→ B   2
→ C   6
→ D   3

8 **When did Maya publish her first book?**
→ A   1981
→ B   1969
→ C   1994
→ D   1950

9 At which president's inauguration did Maya recite her poem "On the Pulse of Morning"?
→ A   Clinton
→ B   Bush
→ C   Obama
→ D   Reagan

10 How many autobiographies did Maya publish?
→ A   2
→ B   3
→ C   7
→ D   5

Answers: 1. A; 2. C; 3. B; 4. D; 5. A; 6. D; 7. C; 8. B; 9. A; 10. C

 Our World

Maya's work and accomplishments still make a difference in our lives. Here are three ways Maya inspires our world today!

→ In 1996, two libraries opened in honor of Maya—the Angelou Branch Library in Stockton, California and the Maya Angelou Northeast Branch Library in Wichita, Kansas. Maya felt most "at home" at the library. Her libraries continue to be homes to others.

→ In 1998, Maya directed *Down in the Delta*. She paved the way for other Black women directors like Ava DuVernay. In 2018, Ava directed *A Wrinkle in Time*. She became the first Black woman to direct a $100 million movie.

→ On January 20, 2021, 22-year-old Amanda Gorman recited her stunning poem "The Hill We Climb" at the inauguration of President Joseph Biden. Like Maya 30 years before, Amanda inspired hope and unity for the nation. Amanda wore a caged bird ring to honor Maya.

Maya was once a young reader like you. What else do you and Maya have in common?

→ Maya had never written an autobiography. She tried anyway and succeeded. Why is it important to try new things?

→ Maya loved reading and writing. She later taught others about words. What is something you love to do and can teach others?

→ Maya learned by reading books. She taught herself how to be a journalist by reading books. How do you learn something new?

Glossary

Arabic: A language spoken by people in the Middle East and North Africa

assassinate: To kill someone, usually a leader, by sudden or secret attack

autobiography: The story of a person's life written by that person

civil rights movement: A time of struggle between 1945 and 1970 when Black people in the United States fought to end racial discrimination and have equal rights

Great Depression: A period of time in history during which people had little money to spend, work was scarce, and many businesses failed. It lasted from 1929 until the late 1930s and affected countries all over the world.

Harlem Writers Guild: An organization of African American writers

inauguration: The ceremony to mark the beginning of something, such as the beginning of a presidency

international: Something that involves many countries

interracial marriage: Marriage between members of different races

mute: Silent or unable to speak

national park: An important park protected by the federal government

porter: A person whose job is to carry customers' luggage for them

producer: A person who raises money and keeps track of spending for a TV show, movie, or play

prudent: Having the quality of thinking before acting

scholarship: Money given to a student to pay for school

segregation: The separation of people, usually based on their race or skin color

Serbo-Croatian: A language spoken in Serbia, Croatia, and the former Yugoslavia

slavery: A system in which people are treated like property and forced to work against their will for no pay

standing ovation: When people stand up to clap for someone

Bibliography

Angelou, Maya. 1969. *I Know Why the Caged Bird Sings*. New York: Random House.

———. 1974. *Gather Together in My Name*. New York: Random House.

———. 1976. *Singin' and Swingin' and Gettin' Merry Like Christmas*. New York: Random House.

———. 1981. *The Heart of a Woman*. New York: Random House.

———. 1986. *All God's Children Need Traveling Shoes*. New York: Random House.

———. 1993. *Wouldn't Take Nothing for My Journey Now*. New York: Random House.

Diepenbrock, George. May 28, 2014. "Experts Available to Speak about Maya Angelou's Life." The University of Kansas. news.ku.edu/2014/05/28/media-advisory-ku-experts-available-speak-about-maya-angelous-life.

Eckels, Carla. June 9, 2014. "Renaissance Woman: Wichitans Reflect on the Life of Maya Angelou." KMUW.org. kmuw.org/arts/2014-06-09/renaissance-woman-wichitans-reflect-on-the-life-of-maya-angelou.

Littleton, Cynthia. May 28, 2014. "Oprah Winfrey on Maya Angelou: 'She Will Always Be the Rainbow in My Clouds.'" *Variety*. variety.com/2014/tv/news/oprah-winfrey-on-maya-angelou-she-will-always-be-the-rainbow-in-my-clouds-1201195062.

Primm, James Neal. 1998. *Lion of the Valley: St. Louis, Missouri, 1764-1980*. St. Louis, MO: Missouri Historical Society Press.

Smithsonian National Museum of African Art. May 28, 2014. "Biography of Maya Angelou." africa.si.edu/2014/05/biography-of-maya-angelou.

Wake Forest University. n.d. "Remembering Dr. Maya Angelou." mayaangelou.wfu.edu/story.

Winfrey, Oprah. n.d. "Oprah: 'Death Shows Up to Remind Us to Live More Fully.'" Oprah.com. oprah.com/spirit/oprah-remembers-dr-maya-angelou_1.

Winfrey, Oprah. n.d. "Oprah Talks to Maya." Oprah.com. oprah.com/omagazine/oprah-interviews-maya-angelou.

About the Author

Tiffany Obeng is a lawyer and author of several educational and inspiring children's picture books. Her books include the popular kids' career books *Andrew Learns about Lawyers* and *Andrew Learns about Engineers*, seasons book *Spencer Knows Spring*, and honesty book *Scout's Honor*. Tiffany has always adored Dr. Angelou and even had the honor of hearing her speak in person. Tiffany truly enjoyed writing this book and hopes young readers have enjoyed it as well.

About the Illustrator

Rahana Dariah is a freelance artist living in Madagascar, her native country. Her passion for kids' literature pushed her to turn it into a living, as she just couldn't consider any occupation other than creating pictures for children. She learned the publishing industry through books and the amazing world of the internet. After working on many independent projects, she managed to build a career as an illustrator, got represented by a reputable agency in 2020, and worked on many titles with most of the major publishers in kids' publishing.

Sawyer loves sunny days and music. She dreams of owning a small cottage and traveling the world. She lives with her family and her two pets, Arya the dog and Potter the cat. Her website is sawyer.cloud.

WHO WILL INSPIRE YOU NEXT?

EXPLORE A WORLD OF HEROES AND ROLE MODELS IN **THE STORY OF**... BIOGRAPHY SERIES FOR NEW READERS.

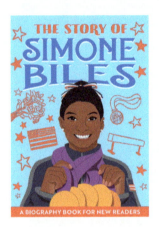
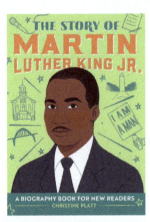

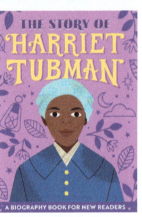

LOOK FOR THIS SERIES
WHEREVER BOOKS AND EBOOKS ARE SOLD

Alexander Hamilton
Albert Einstein
Martin Luther King Jr.
George Washington

Jane Goodall
Barack Obama
Helen Keller
Marie Curie

Printed in the USA
CPSIA information can be obtained
at www.ICGtesting.com
CBHW041526260324
5882CB00005B/27